ANIMAL PREDATORS

Foxes

SANDRA MARKLE

⌐ LERNER PUBLICATIONS COMPANY / MINNEAPOLIS

PREDATORS.

Predators are the hunters that find, catch, and eat other animals—their prey—in order to survive. Every environment has its chain of hunters. The smaller, slower, less able predators become prey for the bigger, faster, more cunning hunters. And everywhere, there are just a few kinds of predators at the top of the food chain. *In nearly every habitat on every continent except Antarctica, this includes one or more kinds of foxes, like this gray fox.*

Foxes are great hunters. They can sneak up on their prey and strike swiftly with sharp teeth. A fox—like this red fox—has a keen sense of smell that helps it find its prey. Its muzzle, all the way from its nostrils to its eyes, is packed with smell-sensitive cells. What it smells shapes a fox's world. Odors can tell a fox what kind of animals have passed by and how long ago they were there.

A fox also depends on another keen sense—hearing. Most foxes, like this bat-eared fox, have big ears that act like sound scoops. Each ear can move separately, turning left, right, up, and down as the fox listens. Their ears can hear sounds too low and too high for human ears to sense—such as the gnawing and squeaking noises mice make. Which ear picks up the sound first and which hears it loudest helps the fox track down the sound's source.

The bat-eared fox lives in the grasslands of Africa where it's very hot year-round. Its ears help it in another way. Blood flowing through its big ears give off some of its body heat to the outside air. This helps the bat-eared fox stay cool.

Once a fox gets close to its prey, its vision helps it make the kill. Most kinds of foxes—like this kit fox hunting in California's Mojave Desert—have catlike pupils, openings at the center of their eyes. Like cats, foxes mainly hunt at night. These kinds of pupils are able to open superwide to let as much light as possible enter. So in very dim light, a fox can easily see shapes and spot movement human eyes would miss.

If it is hungry or if there is an easy chance to catch prey, a fox will also hunt during the day—just as this male red fox in Alaska is doing. Then its pupils close to just slits, cutting down on the amount of light entering its eyes. That keeps the hunter from being blinded by the bright light as it searches for prey.

This male red fox catches the scent of a snowshoe hare. He slows down as the scent becomes stronger. The pads of his feet, even between his toes, are covered with fur to keep them warm. The fur also helps him move nearly silently. Where ice-crusted snow is slick, the fox digs in his sturdy toenails to keep from slipping. When he finally spots the snowshoe hare, the fox lowers his body until his furry belly brushes the snow. He wiggles closer, stalking his prey. But the hare has big ears and big eyes to alert it to danger. The instant the hare senses the fox, it races off.

The male red fox's long hind legs launch him in hot pursuit. For a short distance, these strong hind legs can push him to a speed of nearly 30 miles (48 kilometers) per hour. The fox can run fast even through the deep snow. Because he's so lightweight, he doesn't sink in very deeply. This makes running easier. Streaming behind him, the fox's long, bushy tail helps him keep his balance while he twists and turns.

The snowshoe hare reaches a fallen tree. The hare dives in among spiky branches and escapes. The hungry fox sniffs and waits for a while. Finally, he trots on, searching for easier prey.

This male arctic fox in Norway is searching for prey too.
Arctic foxes live farther north than any other kind of fox. Like red foxes, arctic foxes hunt alone and, during the winter, live alone. That's because the prey they manage to catch is likely to be too small to share.

The arctic fox's fur-soled feet protect his toes from the frozen ground. Arctic foxes are built to keep warm. They have smaller ears, a shorter muzzle, and a thicker, woolier winter coat than other foxes. Come spring, the arctic fox will shed this coat and grow a completely new, thinner, shorter, grayish brown coat. Besides being dressed for the weather, the arctic fox is colored to blend in while hunting in both summer and winter.

The scent of prey the arctic fox has been following becomes even stronger. Then he hears a noise. Homing in on this sound, the arctic fox scratches away the ice crust covering the snow. Then he leaps. His hind legs act like springs, propelling him high into the air.

He dives into the snow, muzzle first, and grabs a lemming, a small Arctic rodent. He bites to make his kill.

Arctic foxes are small, no bigger than an average-sized house cat.
Lemmings are good-sized rodents, weighing nearly 3 ounces (80 grams). A single lemming is a meal for this male fox. After eating, he finds a snowdrift that offers shelter from the icy wind. There he curls up to keep warm, wraps his bushy tail around him like a blanket, and goes to sleep.

Meanwhile, the male red fox is chasing a mouse. While he runs full out, sensitive whiskers and leg hairs help him stay aware of his surroundings. Red foxes often leap and pounce catlike to catch their prey. This time, the red fox thrusts out one foot and traps the mouse.

A fox's slender, curved teeth are made for clamping onto small prey and killing it. He quickly eats the meal he's caught. But one small mouse isn't enough food for a large red fox. Each day, the male red fox needs to catch and eat about a pound (0.5 kilograms) of food.

So the red fox sets off hunting again and comes face-to-face with another male red fox. While most foxes roam year-round, red foxes claim a territory during the breeding season. A territory is an area the fox defends as its home. The male red fox urinated and deposited his wastes at different locations in his territory as scent signposts of his ownership. The invading male is searching for a territory—even if it means fighting for one.

Growling, the rivals charge. The two males rear up on their hind legs as they collide. Their chests slam together. They push at each other with their front paws. They snap their jaws. Each attempts to bite the other. They tumble, roll, and stand. They crash together again. The fight continues until the rival fox runs away yelping.

The male red fox doesn't have to fight any other males that winter. As he continues to hunt, he sometimes crosses paths with a neighbor, a female red fox. She was his mate last year, but for most of the winter, they have ignored each other. Then in early January, the female leaves special scent markings that draw the male fox. When they meet this time, they nuzzle each other.

By late January, the male and female are together most of the time. Because the supply of food is limited during the winter, each hunts for its own food. When the female is ready, the pair mate. Soon babies are developing inside her. So while the female hunts, she also searches for a den, a sheltered spot, under a fallen tree or rocks.

She may choose a den she or other female foxes have used before. Or she may dig a den for herself. Near the end of April, when spring flowers are bursting through the last patches of snow, the female moves into the den she's chosen. There she gives birth to five baby foxes, called pups. (They are also sometimes called kits.) As each is born, she licks it clean. Whimpering, the fuzzy newborns nuzzle into their mother's warm fur. They find a nipple and settle down to nurse.

For the next two weeks, while the pups' eyes remain closed, the female spends most of her time inside the den. The male red fox hunts for them both. Prey is plentiful. Prey animals that stayed in burrows over the winter are active again. Many have had babies. The red fox often brings home rabbits. He even catches several ground squirrels and carries home some to share.

A fox's milk is much creamier than cow's milk. Drinking this rich milk, the pups grow quickly. By the time they are a month old, they often leave the den to play. They chase their tails, wrestle, and play fight. Their rough play helps them become stronger as they become bigger. It also lets the pups practice skills they'll need when hunting or defending prey from other animals.

Though she's never away for long, the female red fox now begins to hunt again. While she's away from the den, the pups explore. When the female returns, she finds one adventurous little male has wandered into the open. She gently but firmly bites him to scold him for leaving the safe den. Other hunters, like eagles or coyotes, are always on the lookout for easy prey, like fox pups.

By the time they are six weeks old, the red fox pups are growing their adult coats. They are starting to look like their parents. The pups are also eating adult food. But even while they were nursing, they gnawed on the prey their father brought home. Chewing this food strengthened their jaws and gave them a taste of their future prey. Now that their mother has stopped letting them nurse, they share their parents' meals.

When their mother arrives with a squirrel, she barks to call the pups. Then she drops the squirrel a little way from the den to encourage the pups to hunt for it. A young male finds the squirrel and runs off with the prize. A sister chases after him to claim her share.

Growing up for a fox is the same the world over. It's all about getting strong enough and clever enough to find and catch prey. While waiting for its parents to bring home food, an arctic fox pup practices pouncing.

A young South African cape fox practices its stalking skills. When it manages to catch a mouse, the tasty meal is its reward.

This red fox pup is hunting alongside its parent. As the pups grow up, the adults often take one youngster with them when they go hunting. The others remain behind at the den. This lets each pup receive some one-on-one training.

By the time autumn arrives, fox families break up. The adults and pups all go their own way. Many small burrowing animals are moving into burrows for the winter, so small prey is harder to find. A family of foxes hunting in the same area means too much competition for meals. Each fox must hunt for itself, so the family needs to spread out. The young males leave first. Eventually, the young females leave too, and the parents separate to hunt alone.

Many young foxes don't survive their first winter. Some fall prey to coyotes or other predators. Some are killed by human hunters or the traps they set. Those that survive perfect their hunting skills.

Young foxes are able to mate and produce young when just ten months old. They need to quickly become expert hunters so they can provide for a family. By spring this young male fox already has a mate and is on the prowl to feed a new generation of hunters.

Looking Back

- What are two ways a fox uses its long, bushy tail? If you need clues, take another look at the foxes on pages 19 and 25.

- Look closely at the young foxes on page 31. A fox's ears can move forward and backward—even separately in two different directions. Check out how the leader in this chase is using its ears to keep track of its rival.

- Compare the red foxes growing up on pages 26, 28, 31, and 34. Besides size, what are some of the ways these youngsters have changed?

Glossary

CLAW: long, sharp-tipped nail on the end of an animal's toe

DEN: place where a fox finds shelter and raises its young

NURSE: to feed on mother's milk

PREDATOR: an animal that hunts and kills other animals in order to live

PREY: an animal that a predator catches to eat

PUP: young fox, sometimes called a kit

PUPIL: the opening at the center of the eye

STALKS: follows prey quietly while hunting

TERRITORY: area in which an animal lives and hunts and is willing to defend from rivals

Further Information

Books

Grambo, Rebecca L. *The World of the Fox*. San Francisco: Sierra Club Books, 1995. Photos and text combine to present fascinating facts about foxes and how they live.

Macdonald, David. *Foxes*. Osceola, WI: Voyageur Press, 2000. Investigate different kinds of foxes in this book.

Matthews, Downs. *Arctic Foxes*. New York: Simon & Schuster, 1995. Photos taken by experts in Arctic exploration and wildlife bring the survival story of arctic foxes to life.

Websites

All about Foxes. http://www.ozfoxes.com/aafoxes.htm
The "Frequently Asked Questions" section on this site makes learning more about foxes fun.

Arctic Fox. http://library.thinkquest.org/3500/arctic_fox.htm
Learn cool facts about arctic foxes and how they live. Listen to the word for "arctic fox" pronounced in the Cup'ik Eskimo language.

Fox Forest. http://www.foxforest.org/
Explore this site to hear the calls of red foxes, see their tracks, and discover lots of fascinating facts about them.

Seasons of the Snow. http://ngm.nationalgeographic.com/ngm/0410/feature4/
See photos and video clips of arctic foxes. Don't miss the behind-the-scenes interview with wildlife photographer Norbert Rosing.

Index

For Matteus, Nathaniel, and Lucy and their parents, Christoph and Jane Zintl

The author would like to thank the following people for sharing their expertise and enthusiasm: Dr. Todd Gosselink, Iowa Department of Natural Resources; and Dr. James Roth, University of Central Florida. The author would also like to express a special thank-you to Skip Jeffery for his help and support during the creative process.

Photo Acknowledgments
The images in this book are used with the permission of: © Alan & Sandy Carey/zefa/CORBIS, p. 1; © Joe McDonald/CORBIS, p. 3; © Staffan Widstrand/CORBIS, p. 4; © Winfried Wisniewski/Minden Pictures, p. 7; © Kevin Schafer/CORBIS, p. 8; © D. Robert & Lorri Franz/CORBIS, p. 9; © Konrad Wothe/Minden Pictures, p. 11; © Tom Brakefield/CORBIS, pp. 13, 20, 23, 35; © Theo Allofs/CORBIS, p. 14; © Rosing, Norbert/Animals Animals, pp. 16, 17; © Eberhard Hummel/zefa/CORBIS, p. 19; © Frank Lukasseck/CORBIS, p. 21; © Alan Carey/Photo Researchers, Inc., p. 24; © Norbert Rosing/National Geographic Image Collection, p. 25; © Andrew Cooper/Minden Pictures, p. 26; © Charles Krebs/Riser/Getty Images, p. 27; © Shin Yoshino/Minden Pictures, p. 28; © Shattil & Rozinski/naturepl.com, pp. 29, 31; © Yva Momatiuk & John Eastcott/Minden Pictures, p. 32; © Peter Lillie/Oxford Scientific Films/Photolibrary, p. 33; © Erwin & Peggy Bauer/Bruce Coleman, Inc./Photoshot, p. 34; © Tim Fitzharris/Minden Pictures, p. 37. Front Cover: © Alan and Sandy Carey/Photodisc/Getty Images.

Lerner Publications Company
A division of Lerner Publishing Group, Inc.
241 First Avenue North
Minneapolis, MN 55401 U.S.A.

Website address: www.lernerbooks.com

Websites listed in Further Reading are current at time of publication

Library of Congress Cataloging-in-Publication Data

Markle, Sandra.
    Foxes / by Sandra Markle.
        p.   cm. — (Animal predators)
    Includes bibliographical references and index.
    ISBN 978-1-58013-536-8 (lib. bdg. : alk. paper)
    1. Foxes—Juvenile literature. I. Title.
QL737.C22M3625 2010
599.775—dc22   2008038090

Manufactured in the United States of America
1 2 3 4 5 6 — DP — 15 14 13 12 11 10